STRANGE
Life Cycles

The Bizarre Life Cycle of a
SALMON

By Mark Harasymiw

Gareth Stevens
Publishing

Please visit our website, www.garethstevens.com. For a free color catalog of all our high-quality books, call toll free 1-800-542-2595 or fax 1-877-542-2596.

Library of Congress Cataloging-in-Publication Data

Harasymiw, Mark.
The bizarre life cycle of a salmon / Mark Harasymiw.
    p. cm. — (Strange life cycles)
Includes index.
ISBN 978-1-4339-7060-3 (pbk.)
ISBN 978-1-4339-7061-0 (6-pack)
ISBN 978-1-4339-7059-7 (library binding)
1. Salmon—Life cycles—Juvenile literature. I. Title.
QL638.S2H24 2013
597.5'6—dc23
                                        2012003228

First Edition

Published in 2013 by
Gareth Stevens Publishing
111 East 14th Street, Suite 349
New York, NY 10003

Copyright © 2013 Gareth Stevens Publishing

Designer: Andrea Davison-Bartolotta
Editor: Kristen Rajczak

Photo credits: Cover, p. © 1 iStockphoto.com/Lee Sutterby; p. 4 Keith Ringland/Oxford Scientific/Getty Images; p. 5 Daniel Cox/Oxford Scientific/Getty Images; p. 7 Natalie Fobes/Photographer's Choice/Getty Images; p. 9 Jeff Foott/Discovery Channel Images/Getty Images; p. 10 © iStockphoto.com/RonTech2000; p. 11 Tohoku Color Agency/Japan Images/Getty Images; p. 13 Klaus Nigge/National Geographic/Getty Images; p. 15 VasikO/Shutterstock.com; p. 16 Richard Seeley/Shutterstock.com; p. 17 © iStockphoto.com/Zixian; p. 19 Keith Douglas/All Canada Photos/Getty Images; p. 20 Vichie81/Shutterstock.com; p. 21 (background) Mansiliya Yury/Shutterstock.com.

Printed in the United States of America

CPSIA compliance information: Batch #CS12GS: For further information contact Gareth Stevens, New York, New York at 1-800-542-2595.

Contents

Words in the glossary appear in **bold** type the first time they are used in the text.

An Incredible Journey

The life cycle of a salmon is truly unbelievable! All salmon begin their life in a stream, lake, or some other body of freshwater. After hatching from eggs, salmon make the long, dangerous journey downstream to the ocean.

After a period of time in the ocean, the salmon make another long journey upstream and return to the same stream or lake where they were born. Those that complete this journey find a **mate**, lay eggs, and die soon after.

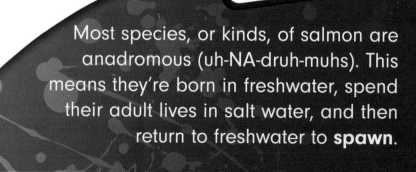

THE FACTS OF LIFE

Most species, or kinds, of salmon are anadromous (uh-NA-druh-muhs). This means they're born in freshwater, spend their adult lives in salt water, and then return to freshwater to **spawn.**

When salmon can't swim past something, they jump over it!

Wide World of Salmon

There are several different species of salmon. The Atlantic salmon is found only in the Atlantic Ocean. It's found throughout the North Atlantic. In European waters, it's found as far south as Portugal. In North American waters, it's found as far south as Maine.

There are also salmon that live in the Pacific Ocean. These are the chinook, chum, coho, pink, and sockeye salmon. Species of Pacific salmon are found in the United States, Canada, Russia, Japan, and Korea.

THE FACTS OF LIFE

Pink salmon were put into the Great Lakes in 1956. Some think this was an accident. They still live there today.

This male sockeye salmon is swimming upstream to find a mate.

Young Salmon

Female salmon lay thousands of eggs in the **gravel** of the stream or lake where they were born. The young salmon, called fry, hatch after several weeks or months, depending on the species. The fry stay in the gravel for a time, living off their **yolk sacs**.

The fry of some species immediately swim to the ocean as soon as they leave the gravel. Other types remain where they hatched for a period of time to feed on **plankton**, insects, and **crustaceans**. These growing salmon are called parr.

THE FACTS OF LIFE

Young Atlantic salmon usually remain where they were born for 1 to 2 years. However, in some places, they remain for up to 8 years before swimming to the ocean!

While salmon fry are attached to their yolk sac, they don't have to eat.

Adulthood

Salmon spend most of their adult life in the ocean. Their bodies change to help them live in salt water. These changes are called smolting.

While in the ocean, salmon feed on small fish, water bugs, and crustaceans. They may stay in the ocean for as few as 2 years, like pink salmon, or as many as 7 years, like chinook salmon. After their time in the ocean, the salmon return to their birthplace to spawn.

Salmon spend their time in the ocean eating to prepare themselves for their long journey to spawn.

The Dangerous Journey Home

Few salmon complete the journey back to their home waters. Some are eaten by other animals. Some die of sickness. Some die on the return journey. That's because most salmon species don't eat on the journey, and many haven't stored enough fat to support themselves.

Once at the spawning grounds, female salmon fight with other females for a good place to lay eggs. Male salmon fight other males to mate with the females.

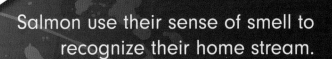

THE FACTS OF LIFE

Salmon use their sense of smell to recognize their home stream.

Only about one in every 1,000 salmon return to the water where they hatched.

13

Life Is Complete

When the female salmon is ready to lay her eggs, she makes a nest called a redd. She uses her fins and tail to make a shallow hole in the gravel. After she lays her eggs in the redd, a male salmon adds cells called milt to them. The female then covers the eggs with gravel.

The female and male do this several more times. In most species of salmon, the male and female die after all the eggs have been spawned.

THE FACTS OF LIFE

Female salmon commonly make four or five redds.

These salmon have made it back to where they were born and are ready to do their part to start the next life cycle.

Salmon Dangers

On their journey back to their birthplace, salmon face hungry animals looking for a fishy meal. Many salmon are caught by bears, otters, and eagles. People like to fish for salmon, too.

Hydroelectric dams across rivers can make salmon's journey hard. Increases in water **temperature** and water pollution can also harm salmon. Because of all of these dangers, salmon have become **endangered** in some areas and completely wiped out in others.

This bald eagle has caught a salmon with the sharp claws on its feet.

Eating salmon is a great way for bears to fatten up before they sleep through winter!

Helping Salmon

People have recognized that salmon need help in parts of their life cycle, especially overcoming man-made problems. To help salmon swim past dams, people have built fish ladders. A fish ladder is a series of pools that salmon jump up into so they can swim up and around the dam. They're somewhat like steps, but for salmon!

People have also helped salmon by setting up hatcheries. Hatcheries are safe places for young salmon to live and find food, water, and space.

THE FACTS OF LIFE

Some salmon swim thousands of miles to reach their home waters. This can take months!

People have made fish ladders like this one to help salmon pass dams.

19

Salmon Farming

Salmon farms are another way people have helped salmon. The more fish are eaten from salmon farms, the fewer wild salmon have to be caught. Young farm salmon are raised in freshwater and then moved to salt water cages when they become adults.

There are downsides to salmon farming, however. Some fish escape the cages and eat wild salmon's food. The large numbers of salmon kept in cages can also lead to illness in the fish. This can spread to nearby wild salmon.

salmon farm

THE FACTS OF LIFE

About 60 percent of the world's salmon lives in fish farms.

Fun Facts About Salmon

Atlantic salmon	Pacific salmon always die after spawning. However, Atlantic salmon may return to the sea after spawning and a year or two later return to spawn again!
chinook salmon	The chinook is the official state fish of Alaska.
chum salmon	Some chum travel more than 2,000 miles (3,200 km) to their spawning streams.
coho salmon	Coho are now found in all the Great Lakes.
pink salmon	Pink salmon are also called humpback salmon or humpy.
sockeye salmon	Some sockeye can find their way using the sun and moon.

Glossary

crustacean: an animal with a hard shell, jointed limbs, feelers, and no backbone

endangered: in danger of dying out

gravel: small pieces of rock and stone

hydroelectric: describing something that produces electricity from the motion of water

mate: one of two animals that come together to make babies. Also, to come together to make babies.

plankton: tiny plants and animals floating in the water

spawn: to produce young, usually in large numbers

temperature: how hot or cold something is

yolk sac: a supply of food surrounding the young of some kinds of animals

For More Information

Books

Catt, Thessaly. *Migrating with the Salmon.* New York, NY: PowerKids Press, 2011.

Jackson, Tom. *Salmon.* Danbury, CT: Grolier, 2008.

Websites

Alaska Department of Fish and Game
www.adfg.alaska.gov/index.cfm?adfg=animals.main
Learn more about salmon as well as other animals living in Alaska.

Salmon of the West
www.fws.gov/salmonofthewest/salmon.htm
Learn about the hardships salmon face during their life cycle and how people can help.

Index